# The Simple Guide to Making Bath Bombs.

*Simple Homemade Natural Recipes for Radiant and Healthy-Looking Skin, Relaxing, Soothing, Rejuvenating, Stress Reduction*

**By Daisy Warren**

# Table of Contents

Bath Bombs. Advantages of DIY Bath Bombs ................................................ 7
   *Ingredients* ........................................................................................... 7
      *Baking Soda and Citric Acid* ............................................................ 8
      *Carrier Oils* ..................................................................................... 9
      *Essential Oils* ................................................................................ 11
      *Modulator* ................................................................................... 11
      *Teas, Herbals, Flowers, and Fruits* .............................................. 14
      *Frosting Recipes* .......................................................................... 16
      *Hard Topping Recipe* ................................................................... 17
      *Soft Topping Recipe* ..................................................................... 17
      *Natural Bubble Frosting* .............................................................. 18
      *Vanilla Spongy Bath Bomb Icing* .................................................. 19
      *Coloring* ....................................................................................... 20

   *Liquid Soap Coloring* ........................................................................ 20
   *Powdered Colorants* ........................................................................ 20
      *Natural Fruit Powders* ................................................................. 21
      *Lemon Peel Powder* .................................................................... 21
      *Orange Peel Powder* ................................................................... 21

*Colored Bath Salts* ............................................................................... *22*
*Cosmetic Clays* ..................................................................................... *22*
*Fruits/Vegetables as Coloring* ....................................................... *22*
Standard Supplies ............................................................................... 24
*Packaging and Storage* ..................................................................... *24*
*Baskets* ................................................................................................ *26*
Basic Bath Bomb Recipe ..................................................................... 27
*Basic Bath Bomb* ................................................................................ *27*
*Basic Bath Bomb 2* ............................................................................ *31*
*Basic Bath Bomb 3* ............................................................................ *31*
*Bath Bombs Secrets &Tips* .............................................................. *32*
*Molding* ................................................................................................ *35*
Recipes Christmas Bath Bomb ......................................................... 38
*Milky Moisture Kick* .......................................................................... *39*
*Super Easy Coconut Oatmeal Bath Bombs* ................................. *40*
*Citrus Bath Bomb* .............................................................................. *41*
*Blueberry &Activated Charcoal Bath Bomb* ............................... *42*
*Cleopatra Milk & Honey Flower Petals Bath Bomb* .................... *43*

............................................................................................................ *44*
*Anti-stress Milk Lavender Bath Bomb* .......................................... *45*

*Mint Treasures ................................................................ 46*
*Wake up Coffee Ylang Ylnag Bath Bomb ........................ 47*
*Coffee and Cream Bath Bomb........................................ 47*
*Chocolate Heaven ......................................................... 48*
*Dead Sea Salt and Cosmetic Clay Bath Bomb ................. 51*
*Anti-Cellulite Green Tea Bath Bombs ............................. 51*
*Milky Bath Bomb ........................................................... 52*
*Vanilla Dream Skin Softening Bath Bombs with Vitamin E .......... 53*
*................................................................................... 54*
*Flower &Herb Bath Bombs ............................................ 55*
*................................................................................... 55*
*Orange Zest Bath Bomb ................................................ 56*
*Chia Seeds Bath Bomb .................................................. 57*

- Disinfecting and Deodorizing Toilet Bath Bombs ....................... 58
- Raspberry and Vanilla Cream Bath Bomb ..................................... 59
- Vanilla Cake Bath Bomb ............................................................ 60
- Pinky Clouds ............................................................................. 62
- Cinnamon Latte Bath Bomb ....................................................... 64
- Velvet Sky ................................................................................. 65
- Healing Freshness ..................................................................... 66
- Sweet Grape Bath Bomb ............................................................ 67
- Ocean Breeze Bath Bomb .......................................................... 69
- Honey and Grapefruit Bath Bomb .............................................. 70
- Tropical Island .......................................................................... 72
- Peppermint Bath Bomb ............................................................. 73
- Autumn Gifts ............................................................................ 74
- Chamomile and Bergamot Relaxation Bath Bomb ...................... 74
- Ginger and Honey Bath Bomb .................................................... 75
- Mulled Wine in Your Bath Tub ................................................... 76
- Strawberry and Vanilla Bath Bomb ............................................ 78
- Japanese Garden ...................................................................... 79
- Floral Patterns .......................................................................... 79
- Hibiscus and Pink Himalayan Salt Bath Bomb ............................ 81

Honey, Oatmeal &Milk Bath Bomb................................................... 83

## Recipes for Children ..................................................................... 84

- Colorful Easter Egg Bath Bomb .................................................. 84
- Good Night My Little Star .......................................................... 86
- Milk and Honey Bath Bomb with a Surprise ............................... 88

Conclusion ........................................................................................ 89

# Bath Bombs. Advantages of DIY Bath Bombs

Bath bombs are mixtures of citric acid, baking soda, essential oils, carrier oils, salt, etc., formed into balls. When this wonderful creation drops into your bathtub water, the combination of baking soda and the citric acid in the balls produces a bubbling effect (also known as effervescing), thus the name "bath bomb." The use of these products is basically to relax, relieve stress, benefit the skin. Bath bombs will also give you an unforgettable aromatherapy experience depending on the essential oil used in the bath bomb.

Today, you can buy bath bombs in many stores. But the problem is, that you never know what is in them, what the ingredients are. And even if you do know what the bath bomb contains the ingredients of this bath product are still not of your choosing. Moreover, they are rather expensive.

And now comes the good news. It is really easy and at least twice as cheap to make bath bombs yourself. All the ingredients are easy to buy, the process is not going to take a lot of your time, and it is also lots of fun to make them. Moreover, the bath bombs are always a good present for your loved ones.

In this book, you will find many wonderful bath bomb recipes, basic ingredients list, and useful tips. So, let us get to the bath bomb making!

**Ingredients**

Where to buy the main ingredients for your bath bomb will depend on where you are residing. Most ingredients you can find in grocery stores, Walmart, Amazon.com and other online stores. Making your bath bombs is very simple and easy, and ingredients are safe. Not only that they make bath time more special, but they can also relax and cleanse. Children are fascinated by them. Adults love the aroma it offers. You can start a small business with your DIY bath bombs or have them as gifts to your family and friends.

The best thing about making them yourself is that you will know exactly what is in them. Not all bath bombs sold out there are all-natural, but you can make all-natural bath bombs at home. DIY bath bombs will also save you at least half the price of what bath bombs cost from artisan shops and bath bomb stores.

### Baking Soda and Citric Acid

Baking soda is the ingredient of a bath bomb which is used almost in all of these bath fizzes. This chemical, also known as bicarbonate of soda or sodium bicarbonate is found in hot springs and mineral springs. It has an exceptional ability to smooth, cleanse, as well as detoxify the skin. Since it is an antacid, it can also be used to relieve indigestion and heartburn.

Citric acid is another basic ingredient for bath bombs making. It is considered to be a weak organic acid which is used as a preservative in many cosmetic companies. Examples of fruits which contain a huge amount of citric acid are lemons and limes. That is because of its capability to repair your skin as well as fortify blood vessels and as a result of the reduction of aging effect. Citric acid also has the ability to remove layers of damaged skin, exposing the healthier skin underneath, and giving your skin a much clearer and younger look.

Both ingredients are inactive when bath bombs are dry, which means that no chemical reaction takes place without water. But as soon as you drop these ingredients into a bath, a chemical reaction occurs. This process creates the fizzles or bubbling effect when you toss the bath bombs into your bath water. This effect also enables the bath bomb to release other healthy ingredients.

Many people ask me if you can make a bath bomb without citric acid. The answer is yes. You can substitute the citric acid with lemon juice or cream of tartar. But be aware of the fact that your bath bombs won't fizz as much. So that's entirely up to you.

**Carrier Oils**

**Olive oil** – a universal oil with antioxidant properties, it is a good moisturizer, makes your skin soft and silky.

**Avocado oil** – helps to regenerate stronger cells, helps the body to repel microbial infections, strengthens your skin. It is full of vitamins E, A and D, beta-carotene and proteins.

**Apricot kernel oil**: cold pressed from dried apricot seeds, this oil penetrates the skin easily, that is why it helps to avoid dryness, irritation; softens and moisturizes the skin.

**Almond oil** – helps against skin rashes and irritation, it is a powerful moisturizer and softener, makes your hair shiny.

**Argan Oil**: is produced from kernels of Marocco Argan tree. This oil is well known for its benefits for skin and hair.

**Cherry Kernel Oil**: is full of vitamin A. It is like Almond oil but not so fatty. This oil is a real vitamin boost for your skin.

**Grapeseed oil** – boosts your skin ability to heal wounds and reduce swelling, wrinkles, stretch marks. This oil is also hypoallergenic.

**Liquid coconut oil** – is a brilliant moisturizer, has an antibacterial and antifungal effect, averts premature aging.

**Jojoba oil** – is an excellent moisturizer, it has a soothing effect, fights against skin irritation, helps against hair loss and premature aging.

**Calendula Oil** – is a great assistant against the inflamed skin, itching, rashes, varicose veins. It also softens and soothes your skin.

**Wheat germ oil** – is high in antioxidants, has an anti-aging effect, assists in collagen production, repairs and heals your skin and hair.

**Macadamia oil** – softens and regenerates the skin, helps to heal wounds, scratches. It is beneficial for soothing your skin.

**Rice Bran Oil** - is good not only for cooking but also for skin care. It is rich in vitamin E and leaves your skin smooth and silky.

**Burdock root oil** – helps to fight against pimples, acne, rashes; promotes natural hair growth; soothes and moisturizes your skin.

**Vitamin E oil** - this oil has a double benefit for your skin. It is both antioxidant and nutrient. It also helps to neutralize free radicals, relieves muscle spasms, treats stretch marks and sunburns, and lightens scars.

**Polysorbate 80** - is a widely used emulsifying agent. It allows mixing water and oils without separating. Polysorbate 80 is particularly handy when it comes to making bath bombs because it extends the bath bomb fizzing time and prevents the oily ingredients from making stains in the bathtub. However, it is not 100% natural, so this up to you to use it or not. It comes in both liquid and powder. You should use Polysorbate 80 to disperse your mica, cocoa powder, and lakes as they're not water-soluble and might stain your bathtub.

## Essential Oils

Although optional, most bath bombs include either an essential oil or fragrance to top off that all-in-one aromatherapy experience. Aromatherapy is the inhalation or therapeutic application of essential oils, which reduce the effects of stress, induce relaxation, and to restore balance to mind, body, and soul. Inhaling relaxing scents or your favorite scents while soaking yourself in warm bath water enhances the feeling of well-being.

## Fragrance Oils

Fragrance oils (also called perfume oils or aromatic oils) are synthetically manufactured oils to reproduce the natural smell of flowers, desserts, fruits, etc. Sometimes they even contain essential oils. They are more affordable than essential oils and have a vast variety of scents.

## Modulator

You can use different types modulators according to your taste and what your skin needs. The modulator is going to slow down the reaction between citric acid and baking soda. You should keep that in mind since sometimes it might be challenging to make bath bombs because the mixture can start bubbling and fizzing before we need it to do so.

Here are some of the modulators that are perfectly suitable for DIY bath bombs and have a variety of features for boosting the skin condition:

**Cream of Tartar** – it helps your bath bombs to harden and also makes them fizz better. The rule of a thumb is adding ½ - 1 Tbsp of Cream of Tartar to 1 cup of Baking Soda.

**Tapioca Starch** – is widely used in cosmetic products as a thickening agent. It also has a detoxifying effect on your skin. If your recipe calls for

Tapioca starch and you don't have any you can substitute it with cornstarch or arrowroot powder.

**Cornstarch** — is frequently used in bath bombs. This ingredient is cheap and easy to buy. Cornstarch also has many benefits for the skin and hair. It works as a natural soother for sunburns, skin irritations, and allergies.

**Cosmetic Clay** — since cosmetic clays are rich in natural minerals and have many valuable properties for our skin and they are frequently used in beauty products. That is why infusing your everyday bath bomb recipes with cosmetic clays is going to be beneficial for your skin. Usually, adding 2-3 tablespoons of this amazing beauty product to your bath bomb is enough to have a positive effect. There are a few types of cosmetic clays that are widely used in a modern cosmetology and SPA procedures. Cosmetic clay helps to harden your bath bombs. The recommended usage is ½ -1 Tbsp per 1 cup of Baking Soda. So, we are going to explain their valuable properties and usage.

**White Clay (Kaolin)** – it is a delicate clay that could be used as a baby powder. It is beneficial for detoxifying the skin and making it smoothed and cleaned.

**Yellow Clay** – this clay can detoxify your skin since it is rich in minerals such as zinc, copper, and potassium.

**Green Clay (Montmorillonite)** – is very rich in minerals and is recommended to use in the treatment of acne, black spots, and oily skin.

**Pink Clay** – is suitable for skin types. It is a powerful cleanser and contains a balanced level of mineral salts, silica and iron oxide.

**Red Clay** – Due to a high level of iron oxide, red clay gets its color. It is not only useful in treating skin irritations but also in improving blood circulation. Like Pink Clay, it also has deep cleansing properties and is suitable for dry, normal and dull skin types.

**Bath Salts** - the benefits of bath salts are uncountable. They contain natural ingredients such as magnesium, potassium, sodium, calcium, etc., that make your skin smooth, soft, and healthy

**Epsom salt** - is the most commonly used in bath salts. This wonderful salt is a natural-occurring mineral with many skincare benefits. It eases and relieves muscle aches, soothes sunburns, exfoliates the skin, smoothing out rough patches, prevents wrinkles, relieves stress and relaxes the body. The magnesium and sulfates found in Epsom salts are easily absorbed through the skin, drawing out toxins from your body, which also helps in reducing restlessness and anxiety. Epsom salts also have anti-inflammatory properties. They can help relieve conditions such as sprains and bruises, athlete's foot, foot odor and fungus, and gout.

**Rice powder** – Asian women have been using rice powder for beauty purposes for a couple of centuries. It has a tremendous impact on our skin. Not only rice powder has an anti-aging effect and amazing oil-absorbing properties, but it also can be used in the treatment of sunburns, oily skin, acne, and even as a whitening agent.

**Milk Powders** – milk powders act as a modulator and a natural foaming agent in a bath bomb. Milk powders are also great for the skin since they soften, sooth and moisturize it. You can use any milk powder you like: skim milk powder, buttermilk powder, goat milk powder, coconut milk powder, etc.

### Teas, Herbals, Flowers, and Fruits

**Orange Peel Powder** – has a natural citrus aroma and is full of vitamins and minerals. Interestingly, orange peel has more Vitamin C than the flesh of this fruit. This powder can be easily made at home. Just dry orange peels for a couple of days and then crush them in a blender or a food processor. Orange peel powder should be kept in an airtight container or jar.

**Lemon Peel Powder** – is loaded with vitamins and antioxidants. Lemon peel powder has been proved to be successful in treating varicose veins. You can also make it at home. Just peel off strips of zest with a vegetable peeler and let them dry for a couple of days. When completely dried crush them with a blender or food processor.

**Grapefruit Peel Powder** – has a wonderfully fresh aroma. It is full of the nutrients for your skin such as Vitamin C, iron, potassium and antioxidants. It is known to help our skin to produce collagen and regenerate skin cells. Using this powder for bath bombs making has one more advantage: it is a good natural colorant. Making orange peel powder at home is simple. Peel off zest and dry it for a few days and the crush these peels in a food processor or blender.

**Chamomile Flowers** – has lots of benefits for our skin. It helps to treat acne, spots, and scars. This simple looking flower is also loaded with antioxidants and can protect our skin from free radicals. You can use dry flowers or chamomile flowers powder in bath bombs making.

**Rose Petals and Buds** – rose compounds can brighten up your skin, moisturize it and, moreover, protect it from pollutants. Your skin will get smoother and softer. And since rose also has some therapeutic benefits taking a bath with the rose petals will result in stress reduction and relaxing.

**Lavender Flowers** – is known for its amazing benefits such as stress reduction, relaxing, improving your mood, promoting good sleep. Dried lavender flowers can help to reduce irritations, lower inflammations, eliminate swelling and dandruff. That is why they are widely used in natural cosmetics and herbal remedies.

**Calendula Flowers** – it also is known as Marigold Calendula flowers are a perfect remedy for irritated skin and oil contained in these flowers is especially good for wound healing.

**Mint** – is famous for its relaxing benefits, relieving muscle pain and general calming effect on the body.

**Oatmeal (ground) or Colloidal Oats** – is useful for soothing skin and calming rashes, inflammations and burns. It's a perfect ingredient for a Honey and Oatmeal Bath Bomb.

**Comfrey Powder** – is famous for its pain relieving and wound healing abilities.

## Foaming Agents

**Sodium Lauryl Sulfoacetate (SLSA)** – is a surfactant of a natural origin as it is made from palm and coconut oil. It is one of the most gentle foaming agents. It creates bubbles which last longer, and it prolongs the fizzing time of your bath bomb substantially. However, if you add too much of this product to your batter, you will get a very slow moving bath bomb. Just keep in mind that SLSA is airborne so when you work with it can make you cough. Take precautions and do not forget to put your mask on.

**Sodium Lauryl Sulfate (SLS)** – is a surfactant which produces a luxurious foam and bubbles but it does not have a good reputation. However, most of the shampoos we use contain it. It is entirely up to you to use it or not. SLSA is a perfect substitution for SLS in your bath bomb recipes.

**Milk Powders** – are a natural substitution for SLS and SLSA. Buttermilk powder is going to add more foam to your bathtub than other, other milk powders.

# The Simple Guide to Making Bath Bombs.

**Frosting Recipes**

    Today you can find bath bombs of every shape and color. Lately, cupcake bath fizzes have become very popular. No wonder, they look so tasty and colorful. When it comes to making cupcake bath bomb base, you will find no difficulties. You can choose whatever recipe this book provides and go on and make them. However, real cupcakes come with frosting, so do cupcake bath bombs. So here are some useful recipes for fizzes frosting or topping which you can use for a variety of bath treasures.

### Hard Topping Recipe

**Ingredients:**

200 gr white soap base

liquid color

cosmetic glitter

INSTRUCTIONS:
1. Over a medium-heat melt 200 gr of the white soap base.
2. Once the base is completely melted, add food colorant of your choosing and whisk with an electric whisk until this mixture gets light and airy. As the soap mixture cools down, it will have smooth, creamy consistency.
3. Now you can spoon the mixture and place it on top of the bath bombs covering upper part.
4. Sprinkle the topping with a little bit of cosmetic glitter.
5.

### Soft Topping Recipe

**Ingredients:**

200 gr Foaming Bath Butter or Icecream Soap

liquid color

flower petals (fresh or dried)

INSTRUCTIONS:
1. Over a medium-heat melt 200 gr of the white soap base.
2. Once the base is completely melted, add food colorant of your choosing and whisk with an electric whisk until this mixture gets light and airy. As the soap mixture cools down, it will have smooth, creamy consistency.
3. Now you can spoon the mixture and place it on top of the bath bombs covering upper part.
4. Sprinkle the topping with some flower petals.

# The Simple Guide to Making Bath Bombs.

## Natural Bubble Frosting

**Ingredients:**

3 cups baking soda

1 ½ cup citric acid

½ cup fine grain bath salt

1 cup cornstarch

3 tbsp cream of Tartar

½ cup powdered milk

Rosemary essential oil (or any other essential oil of your choosing)

1 cup cocoa butter

½ cup liquid glycerine (if you do not have any you can replace glycerine with liquid soap)

3 egg whites

Piping bag

Decoration (dried flower petals, dried lemon or orange pieces, cosmetic glitter, colorful bath salt, etc.)

INSTRUCTIONS:

1. Mix baking soda, citric acid, powdered milk, cornstarch, 2 tablespoons of cream of Tartar and bath salt in a large bowl.
2. Add a few drops of essential oil to the dry mixture. Set aside.
3. Whisk egg whites and 1 tablespoon of cream of Tartar until stiff. You can use a hand mixer as well.
4. Pour in glycerine or liquid soap and mix whisk it one more time.
5. Melt cocoa butter and add it to the dry mixture and mix well until it has a mushy consistency. The butter should be slightly warm.
6. Now it is time to add egg whites mix to the mixture. Keep in mind, that it is important to add egg whites mix a little bit at a time. You might not need all of it so just add it until you get a wished consistency.
7. Fill up a piping bag with the mixture.
8. Start frosting you bath bomb cupcakes and do that quickly because this mixture dries fast. Tipp: if you notice that icing is expanding too much add a little bit of baking soda and mix it again.

Once you have frosted your cupcakes, sprinkle them with dried flower petals or bath salts of different colors. Feel free to experiment, and you can find even better ideas to decorate bath bomb cupcakes.

Let them dry until the frosting is hard. It usually takes up to 24 hours.

**Vanilla Spongy Bath Bomb Icing**

This frosting recipe is easy to make, and it looks great on DIY bath bombs and soaps. Moreover, it will create more bubbles in your bathtub once you put in the water. The frosting does not get that "hard as a rock" texture. However, bath products frosted with this icing will need 2-3 days to dry enough so you can pack them.

**Ingredients:**

1 cup foaming bath base (Foaming Bath Whip)

1 cup detergent free clear melt and pour soap base

3 tbsp meringue powder

1 tbsp liquid glycerine or liquid soap

10 drops vanilla essential oil

Yellow liquid colorant (you can use a different color if you want)

Cosmetic glitter or some herbals for decoration

INSTRUCTIONS:

1. Melt soap base in a microwave and let it cool down for a few minutes.
2. In a large bowl mix foaming bath base, meringue powder, glycerine, and vanilla essential oil. It is important to stir it first with a spoon or spatula.
3. Add a few drops of liquid colorant and mix it on medium with a mixer.
4. You should mix the mixture for 1-2 minutes.
5. Now pour in clear melt and pour soap base. Turn the mixer on high and mix the mixture two more minutes.
6. When the mixture gets stiff, then it is ready to use.
7. Place the mixture in a piping bag and frost your bath bombs.
8. Decorate them with cosmetic glitter or some herbals.

## Coloring

Liquid Soap Coloring

It is best to put in some liquid colorant first before adding water to the mixture. The liquid colorant can also help you get the right consistency, so be mindful of the amount of colorant you apply to your mixture. The more liquid colorant you add, the wetter your batter will get which can lead to a premature reaction between citric acid and baking soda. You should only choose FDA approved dyes if you consider selling your bath bombs

### Powdered Colorants

**Lakes** - lakes are water-insoluble colorants that is why most of the manufacturers recommend using Polysorbate 80 with it to disperse this powder and to prevent your bath fizzy from staining your bathtub. You should only choose FDA approved lakes if you consider selling your bath bombs.

**Mica** – is a fine sparkly powder which helps to color your bath bombs. It is recommended to use Polysorbate do disperse your mica when you make bath bombs. Mica can give your bath bombs a nice pastel color. But if you're looking for vibrant color, then you should take a look at lakes and water-soluble dyes.

**Water soluble dyes** – water-soluble dyes are going to color your water and give a vibrant color to your bath bomb. You do not use any Polysorbate 80 with these dyes.

## Natural Fruit Powders

We have already mentioned a few powdered colorants in the chapter "Teas, Herbals, Flowers, and Fruits." ***However, in this chapter, we are going to look at them from a different perspective.***

### Lemon Peel Powder

Lemon peel powder can be used for many reasons. It can be used for skin whitening, facial cleansing, and the oily skin treatment, as well as reducing pimples in acne prone skin.

Lemon peel powder can be purchased online or can be made at home. To make lemon peel powder, you need a peeler, grinder, and food dehydrator. Peel the lemon using a peeler and put the peels in the dehydrator. The temperature setting will depend on the type of dehydrator you are using and is mentioned in the instruction form provided. For some, it might take around 24 hours for the lemon peels to dehydrate completely. Then you can grind the lemon peels to make a powder. Be sure to dry the peels completely before you grind them.

### Orange Peel Powder

Orange peel powder has many natural properties that will heal, protect, and maintain beautiful facial skin. You can use it as a natural cleanser, natural astringent, toner, and to improve circulation.

To make orange peel powder, thoroughly wash 3 to 4 medium-sized oranges and pat dry using a cotton cloth. Peel the oranges using a sharp knife. Do not include the white part of the skin when cutting. As much as possible, get the top layer only. Cut the peels into thin slices so that they dry faster. Put the peels on a tray and place under the sun to dry. Be sure to cover the tray to prevent insects and dust from getting into contact with them. A net can be used or a thin cloth as a covering. Once completely dry, put all the dried peel into a food processor. Make sure that the food processor is completely dry because any amount of moisture can spoil the powder. Grind into a fine powder by blitzing on high speed for about 25 seconds or until it is finely powdered.

### Colored Bath Salts

You can also use ready bath salts for colorant your bath bombs. They come in different colors and sometimes even contain some carrier and essential oils.

### Cosmetic Clays

Another way to color the bath bombs without actually adding a colorant is to use cosmetic clays. The most common cosmetic clays are green, yellow, red, and pink.

### Fruits/Vegetables as Coloring

If you are trying to stay away from those store-bought colorings yet still want to make colorful bath bombs, these chemical-free ideas are for you.

Colors:

Red – use raspberries, pure pomegranate juice or roasted beets.

Yellow – use raw carrots, lemon peel powder, or mangoes.

Blue – use radicchio or red cabbage.

Orange – orange peel powder, curry powder

### *INSTRUCTIONS:*

Make one color at a time.

**Fruits:**

For raspberries (red) or ripe mango (yellow), start the process with a cup of fresh or frozen fruit. Put it all in a blender, until the liquid becomes thick. Strain the thick liquid to take out all the seeds. The outcome should be about a half cup of juice.

**Root vegetable:**

For roasted beets (red) or raw carrots (yellow), a juicer is needed to extract all the juice without any pulp. Use one whole beet and two large carrots, or you can use 1 cup of either one, chopped up. You can choose to use either a food processor or a juicer, pouring in just enough water to make a liquid mixture. Just add a touch of water until you have enough to blend the veggies completely. After that, strain the liquid to remove the pulp. The outcome will depend on how big the vegetable you are using, but for this method, it should be about half a cup of juice.

**Cabbage:**
For radicchio or red cabbage (blue), choose only one between the two and cut up a small head then add to a medium-sized pot and cover with water. Bring to a boil and simmer for about 25 minutes or until the water turns deep purple. Take out the cabbage, strain the liquid, and add 1/4 teaspoon of baking soda. The liquid should turn to blue.

Once you have the colored liquid, you will have to reduce it to make a more powerful colorant agent. Pour the juice into a saucepan and simmer over medium heat until you achieve a thick, very colorful mixture.

You can store the excess paste by pouring them into ice cube molds and letting it freeze. You can also use them for frostings, dough, or batter for baking. But remember, a little should go a long way.

## Standard Supplies

Besides the bath bomb ingredients, you will also need some tools which are going to be helpful.
- a large mixing bowl
- measuring spoons, cups
- digital scale
- whisk
- gloves
- spritzer/spray bottle
- large strainer
- parchment paper and plastic wrap
- an airtight container or a jar
- cello bags for wrapping
- bath bomb molds
- plastic wrap

If you do not have bath bomb molds at home, you can experiment with cupcake tins, meatball maker, soap, ice, or candy molds of various shapes and sizes.

## Packaging and Storage

If you can DIY your bath bombs, you can DIY your bath bomb storage as well! In storing bath bombs, one essential thing that you always should remember is to maintain their freshness. There are tons of ideas on how you can store bath bombs while keeping them fresh and fancy. Browse over below for some of our suggestions on storing bath bombs.

**DIY Bath Bomb Storage Ideas:**

<u>Plastic Bags</u>

Remove air from the plastic bag as much as possible. Seal the plastic bag by tying a knot right above the bath bomb and use scissors to cut off the excess part of the plastic bag.

Store them individually. Putting more than one bath bomb in a plastic bag will cause them to bump into each other and break down.

Store in a cool, dark place. Put your individually-wrapped bath bombs in an air-tight container or any jars with a lid. Keep them in a bathroom cabinet or closet to keep them away from heat, light, and moisture.

<u>Plastic Wraps</u>

This storage idea is one of the efficient ways of keeping bath bombs fresh and free from moisture. Seal each bath bomb separately, making sure that there are no spaces around the bath bombs. Sealing them one by one will keep them from crumbling.

<u>Glass Containers</u>

Glass containers can make such a classy decoration in a bathroom. You can get the illusion of less clutter from the clear glass, and bath bombs do make an alluring piece of decor for the eye. Considering of course that bath bombs are sealed in plastic bags or plastic wraps before putting them inside the glass containers.

Cupcake Stands

If you plan to use your bath bombs more often, you can leave them on cupcake stands without wrapping them in plastics. Not only that they make such lovely bathroom decoration, but they will also make your room smell good. However, you can also wrap the bombs individually in plastics before putting them on cupcake stands. If you are using cupcake tins for making bath bombs, then you might find it useful to place the DIY fizzes in the real cupcake paper cases which will make your bath treasures look even more convincing.

## Baskets

Putting your bath bombs in baskets is a great idea too. There are lots of basket designs out there. You can choose to line the bottom of the basket with linen or paper, or maybe with aluminum wrap foil. Additionally decorating them with some flowers or dried fruit pieces will also look wonderful and will add some freshness to the bathroom.

### Egg Container or Egg Carton

This one of the cheapest and the most creative way to store your bath bombs. You can also decorate an egg container with ribbons and some stickers, paint them in different colors.

### Shrink Wrapping

You will need a heat gun and an impulse sealer to shrink wrap your bath bombs. This type of packaging is more of a professional way to handle your products. It is perfect for those who want to sell their bath bombs, but people who make their bath bombs for personal use tend to enjoy shrink wrapping their bath and body products as well because it keeps their bath treats last longer.

## Basic Bath Bomb Recipe

When it comes to a basic bath bomb recipe, then the most important thing is proportion. Baking soda and citric acid proportion should be 2:1. You can also add other ingredients such as milk powder (for foam), SLSA (it gives bubbles and makes your bath bomb fizz longer), cream of tartar (hardens your bath bomb). After you learn how to make a bath bomb following the basic recipe you can experiment with different ingredients, shapes, and colors.

**Basic Bath Bomb**

**Ingredients:**

½ cup Citric acid

1 cup baking soda

¾ cup cornstarch (rice powder/cosmetic clay/tapioca starch/)

1/4 cup Epsom salts (bath salts)

2 tbsp carrier oil

Colorant (optional)

Binder (water/witch hazel/rubbing alcohol)

Dried flowers (optional)

Fragrance oil or Essential oil (the amount depends on how strong you want your bath bombs to smell. Make sure not to put more than the manufacturer recommends)

The Simple Guide to Making Bath Bombs.

INSTRUCTIONS:
1. Gather all the ingredients.

2. Combine all the dry ingredients and sift them. In a large mixing bowl, add the citric acid, baking soda, and cornstarch. Whisk thoroughly.

*Optional: You can add ¼ cup of Epsom salt after mixing all the ingredient.*

3. Mix your oils with your essential oils or fragrance oils. Add a small amount oil per time. Mix very well until your mixture has big clumps in it.

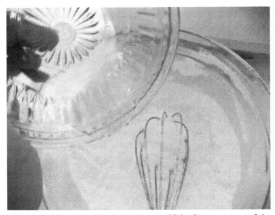

4. Add your binder. The amount of binder you need is going to depend on the humidity level and your ingredients. Use a spray bottle to dampen the mixture you've just created. Add water enough to make the batter moldable. When you squeeze some mixture in your hand, it should keep its shape.

   *Note: Adding too much water will make the mixture bubbly and reacting prematurely. If this happens, add some baking soda or cornstarch to your mixture.*

   *Tip: After spritzing the mixture two or three times, give it another stir using your hands. It should have the consistency of wet sand and hold together well. If it doesn't, add a little more liquid and try again.*
   *Tip: You can mix in multiple scents and colors to create a unique combination.*

5. Fill in your molds with your mixture. Press the mixture firmly into the molds, to prevent them from cracking if you use silicone molds. If you use round bath bomb molds, then sprinkle your mixture in both halves of your mold, overfill them with the batter as much as

you can and press them together. Slightly tap with a spoon to release your bath bomb.

*Tip: If you want to make smaller bath bombs, you can use silicone candy molds.*

6. Let the bombs dry. Leave them in the molds for at least 24 hours if you use silicone molds. It is advisable to place the molds in a cool, dry area away from moisture. If after 24 hours, the bath bombs are still slightly damp, carefully remove them from the molds and allow them to air dry. If it is humid where you live then, you should put them in an airtight container with some rice in it to absorb the moisture. If you use round plastic or aluminum molds take your bath bombs out right away.
7. Store the bath bombs. When the bath bombs are finally dry, remove them from the drying area and store them in a hermetic container or a glass jar. Keep the bombs away from moisture to prevent premature fizzing.

*Tip: It is better to use the bath bombs within a few months, as they do not contain any preservatives.*

**Basic Bath Bomb 2**
    1 cup Baking Soda
    ½ cup Citric acid
    1/4 cup cornstarch
    ½ cup Epsom Salts
    1 tbsp Cream of Tartar
    1 tbsp Cosmetic Clay
    2 tbsp oil
    Colorant
    Binder (water/witch hazel/rubbing alcohol)

**Basic Bath Bomb 3**

    1 cup Baking Soda
    ½ cup Citric Acid
    ½ tbsp. Cream of Tartar
    ½ tbsp. Kaolin Clay
    1.5 tbsp light oil
    Binder (water/witch hazel/rubbing alcohol)
    Fragrance
    Colororant

## Bath Bombs Secrets & Tips
### Humidity

Consider the humidity when you make bath bombs. A day with humidity between 40%-50% would be ideal for bath bomb making. In cases when humidity is high with some percentage of rain showers, the salt incorporated in the bath bombs may soak up the moisture from the air which can cause premature fizzing. It's always a bad idea to make bath bombs if it's raining. However, if you live in a place where it's always humid, but you are in love with bath bombs, then you might want to use it rubbing alcohol 91% as your binder. Another solution to this problem is running a dehumidifier.

<u>Binder</u>

Water – you can use water as your binder if it is pretty dry where you live. I use water when the humidity in my house is not higher than 50%.

*Witch hazel* – witch hazel contains a lot of water that is why I recommend using it when the humidity level is not higher than 50%.

*Rubbing alcohol 50 %-70* - you can also use it in dry and medium humid climates.

*Rubbing alcohol 91% or higher* – you should use in a very humid climate. If you use this binder in a dry climate, your mixture might not shape well, and your bath bombs will become powdery.

### Getting the right consistency:

When your mixture is too wet, then it has a dough-like texture that sticks to your fingers with a loud hissing or crackling sound. In this case, your bath bomb will expend out of the molds. You can save the batch like this by adding more cornstarch and baking soda and mixing with a hand mixer on the highest speed. When your mixture is too dry, it is going to have a hard or crumbly texture that slips through your fingers like sand and will not keep its shape when squeezed in your hand.

Here is the main steps of the bath bomb making procedure which will help you to get the right consistency for your bath bomb. Once you learn to feel your mixture, it is only going to go uphill for you.

**To avoid clumps**, you should sieve all of your dry ingredients. If you want a very smooth bath bomb, then you should grind your citric acid (if it is coarse) and Epsom salts or whatever salt you are using as they tend to make clumps. You can grind them in a coffee grinder or a food processor. If you are a beginner, then you might find it easier to use Granulated Citric Acid. But your bath bombs will have a better texture and look if you use Powdered Citric Acid. However, keep in mind that in this case, the bath bombs might "grow" too soon.

Make sure that the percentage of the carrier and essential oils in the recipe is right. Putting too much of oil can cause the bath bombs to remain soft instead of hardening. **The rule of a thumb is 1 tbsp of a carrier oil per 1 cup of your main dry ingredients.**

Once all of your dry ingredients are presifted, it is time to add your oils. Slowly pour in your oils and mix with your hands. This part does take a while; you should really make sure that your oils are well incorporated into your dry ingredients. **You should mix in your oils until you get a soft clump.** What does it mean, Daisy? – You are going to ask me. It means that the mixture is going to get very clumpy with some big clumps in it, and when you squeeze some of the mixture in your hand it kind of holds its shape, but it is still very easy to break. There is a test you can make. Make a

# The Simple Guide to Making Bath Bombs.

clump in your hand and drop it in the bowl with your batter. It is going to break or crumble. Only after you have achieved this consistency, you can start adding your binder.

Depending on your humidity you are going to use a different binder. Some people put their binder in a spray bottle. I prefer using a dropper because in this way I can see how much liquid I am actually using. You can use a kitchen aid machine or a hand mixer or mix with your hands. Just keep in mind that you should add a little bit of a binder per time and mix vigorously to prevent your ingredients from fizzing prematurely. **The right consistency feels like damp sand or fluffy snow**

You are going to notice that your batter also feel cool. When you now make a clump and drop it down it is going to keep its shape. You can also toss it from one hand to another without breaking it. It means that your mixture is ready to be molded.

If your bath bomb mixture dries out too fast, then you might have to add some more liquid in between. I have to do that as well. You can also cover your mixing bowl with a towel or a piece of plastic wrap to keep your batter from drying up.

Start the recipe with two parts baking soda to 1 part of citric acid plus half of the modulators, such as cornstarch, rice flour, clay, or salt. The modulator will hamper the chemical reaction between the citric acid and the baking soda. This method is going to give you enough time to mix in the liquid.

Try to refrain from using liquid food colorings until you have practiced enough with the basic recipe. You can add a water-based color to the alcohol in the spritz bottle.

If you see that your mix activates and it is difficult for you to find this perfect moldable consistency you might want to try **adding your citric acid last.** So you mix all of your dry ingredients with your oils and your binder until your batter forms a big clump, and then you add your citric acid.

Some of you might also make some homemade soap. For those, who do here is an idea. Make some tiny soaps in different shapes and place them on the top of the bath bombs before they set. This small decoration pieces will make your fizzes look creative and original.

Citric acid tends to take off nail polish, so wear gloves to protect your manicure and avoid skin irritation. If you make bath bombs for sale, then you should wear gloves for sure.

**Molding**
Depending on the molds you use your packing technique is going to be different.

# The Simple Guide to Making Bath Bombs.

Silicone molds – if you use silicone molds you have to pack tightly so your bath bombs will not crack. You should also leave your bath fizzies to dry completely before taking them out.

Round molds - when you use round molds then you should pack lightly. If you pack your molds too tight, the bath bombs will sink. If that is not the problem for you, then it is going to be easier for you. Overfill your two halves of the mold as much as you can and push them together. Then lightly tap on the mold to help to release your bath bomb. Once your bath bombs are unmolded lightly press your finger on the bath bomb surface. If it leaves a dent, then your bath fizzies are not packed tight enough, and you should either remold them completely or sprinkle a little bit of a mixture on the bottom of the half of the mold and push the two halves of the mold

together again.

Baking Tray – you can leave your bath bombs to dry completely before unmolding them or unmold them after 5-10 minutes. You might want to cover the bottom of the tray with a towel and then tap with a spoon until your bath bombs are released.

**Spinning and Floating**

You should focus on making a rock hard bath bomb first if you are a beginner. Once you are happy with the way, your bath bombs look you can start working on how they act. A bath bomb floats when it is light. So if you use too much salt, then you might have a problem with floating. Make sure you pack your molds lightly and always keep your mix fluffy and airy. I use a hand mixer to introduce some air to my mix.

Once you get a floater, you can start working o spinning. When you fill up your molds poke three holes in your mixture. These air holes are going to make your bath bomb lighter and when one part of your bath bombs has it and the other one does not it is going to make your bath fizzies to spin.

Another way to get a floater is to poke a hole with your finger right in the middle of your mixture when you are molding.

## Recipes
### Christmas Bath Bomb
This bath bomb with clove essential oil and vanilla extract will bring you to Christmas mood.

**Ingredients:**

1 cup baking soda

2 tbsp Sweet Almond Oil

½ cup cornstarch

1/2 cup citric acid

5 drops of lavender essential oil

4 drops of clove essential oil

3 drops of vanilla extract

colorant

Fragrance oil (if you don't want to use essential oils)

binder

Molds

INSTRUCTIONS:
1. First, mix dry ingredients (corn starch, citric acid, and baking soda).
2. Then add essential oils or fragrance oil to almond oil.
3. Slowly add liquid ingredients to the dry mixture and mix it until it forms a soft clump. It should stick together and shape well.
4. Add enough binder to get the consistency similar to the wet sand.
5. Oil your molds with a few drops of oil and lightly dust them with cornstarch to avoid sticking.
6. Stuff it into your molds and push your molds together.
7. Unmold and let them dry for at least 24 hours before unmolding.

## Milky Moisture Kick

If your skin is dry and needs some boost, this homemade bath bomb recipe was created for you. It will give your skin what it was longing for. After taking a bath with the Moisture Kick Milk Bath Bomb, your skin will be as smooth as silk. This bath bomb also has a relaxing and soothing effect.

Ingredients:

1 cup baking soda

1/2 cup citric acid

1/4 cup   cornstarch

1/8 cup   bath sea salt  or Epsom salt (finely ground)

1/3 cup   powdered milk

1 Tsp.  liquid coconut oil

1 Tsp. cocoa butter

1 Tbsp.  almond oil

1tsp. rose essential oil

1tsp. lavender essential oil

1 Tbsp. dried rose petals

Pink coloring

Binder


INSTRUCTIONS:
1. Combine all the dry ingredients thoroughly in a large bowl.
2. Put all the wet ingredients into a plastic container and then place it into a microwave until cocoa butter melts.
3. Wait a few minutes until the mixture cools down a little bit.

# The Simple Guide to Making Bath Bombs.

4. Add colorant to the dry mixture and stir to incorporate the ingredients.
5. Add slowly liquid ingredients to the dry mixture and mix. Continue to pour liquid ingredients into the bowl with dry mixture and mix everything until you get a soft clump.
6. Then add your binder until your batter has the consistency of wet sand and shapes well.
7. Pack the mold firmly and avoid making gaps.
8. Leave them in your molds for a few minutes.
9. Then carefully take them out and let them dry overnight.

Tipp: you can spray bath bombs with floral water or witch hazel water or with a mixture of witch hazel water and floral water, so they don't break apart and stick together better.

**Super Easy Coconut Oatmeal Bath Bombs**

These wonderful bath bombs are going to be a special bonus to your bath. When you put one of these bath jewels in the water, it will release the magical natural aroma into the air and fill your bath with nourishing oils that are going to moisturize and cleanse your skin.

**Ingredients:**

1/8 cup colloidal oats

1 cup baking soda

1/4 cup sea salt

½ cup citric acid

1 tbsp cornstarch

1 tbsp Kaolin Clay or Cream of Tartar

2 Tbsp. Virgin coconut oil

Essential oils or fragrance oil (about ½-1 tbsp)

molds

INSTRUCTIONS:
1. Combine colloidal oats, baking soda, citric acid and sea salt with a whisk thoroughly.
2. Melt coconut oil until completely liquid. Microwave works great.
3. Let it cool down for a few minutes.
4. Slowly pour coconut oil into the bowl with dry ingredients while mixing.
5. Add your binder and mix quickly. The mixture should have a consistency that packs well together.
6. Pack your molds with the mixture and wait a few minutes.
7. Take the bath bombs out carefully.
8. Let them dry for 24 hours before using.

**Citrus Bath Bomb**

This natural bath bomb will enrich your experience in bath taking, refresh your skin and mind, relax your body. Orange peel powder is rich in

# The Simple Guide to Making Bath Bombs.

skin-boosting ingredients and is well known for its beneficial influence on skin. Citrus oils of orange and lemon are going to fill up your bathroom with unforgivable fruity scent. And a happy orange color will bring peace and creativeness you're your day.

**Ingredients:**
1 cup baking soda
½ cup citric acid
1/4 cup cornstarch

1 tbsp. orange peel powder
¼ cup sea salt
2 Tbsp. Almond oil
½ tsp. orange essential oil

¼ tsp. lemon essential oil (or fragrance oil)
binder as necessary

Orange food colorant or some curry powder

INSTRUCTIONS:
1. Place the dry ingredients in a bowl and then whisk ingredients until mixed thoroughly.
2. Whisk liquid ingredients.
3. As you put the wet ingredients in the dry mixture whisk, mix it immediately to avoid clumps.
4. Add your binder a little bit per time and mix quickly. Add your binder and mix until your mixture has the consistency similar to the wet sand and feels cool.
5. Mold your bath bombs.
6. Set aside for a few minutes.
7. Pop the bath bombs out.
8. Let them try for 24 hours.
9. Store these bath bombs in an airtight container, jar or wrap them with plastic wrap.

**Blueberry & Activated Charcoal Bath Bomb**
Since activated charcoal is getting more and more popular in the field of beauty products we have decided to create a bath bomb which would possess the wonderful benefits of this unusual ingredient. This Activated Charcoal Bath Bomb with coconut oil and blueberry powder will detox your skin, enrich it with antioxidants and leave a gentle fragrance of bergamot and lime on your skin and hair.

**Ingredients:**

1 cup baking soda

½ cup citric acid and additionally

1 Tbsp. activated charcoal (finely ground)

1 tbsp Kaolin Clay

1.5 Tbsp. melted coconut oil

5 drops bergamot essential oil (or fragrance oil)

10 drops lime essential oil (or fragrance oil)

1 tsp blueberry powder

witch hazel water/water/rubbing alcohol (a binder)

INSTRUCTIONS:
1. Combine baking soda, citric acid, blueberry powder and fine ground activated charcoal. Mix well.
2. Pour melted coconut oil into the bowl and add your fragrance.
3. Mix until you get a soft clump.
4. Add your binder a little bit per time and mix quickly. Add your binder and mix until your mixture has the consistency similar to the wet sand and feels cool.
5. Mold your bath bombs and carefully take them out. You might have to tap a little bit.
6. Let them dry for 24 hours.

**Cleopatra Milk & Honey Flower Petals Bath Bomb**

## The Simple Guide to Making Bath Bombs.

Cleopatra was the flower of Ancient Egypt which was known for her beauty and cleverness. One of her secrets was taking milk baths infused with honey and fine herbs. One more way to get the benefits of Cleopatra milk bath is to make this amazing nourishing bath bomb with honey and flower petals. Your skin will get a silky smoothness and healthy glow.

Ingredients:

1 cup baking soda

½ cup citric acid

1/8 cup cornstarch

¼ cup powdered milk

1.5Tbps. Argan oil

1 tbsp honey powder or ½ tbsp. warm honey

Fragrance (fragrance oil or essential oil)

Binder as necessary

2 Tbsp. dried flowers (rosebuds, dried chamomile, calendula, lavender, etc.).

INSTRUCTIONS:
1. Place the dry ingredients in a bowl and then whisk ingredients until mixed thoroughly.
2. Slowly add well-combined honey, fragrance and argan oil to the dry mixture and mix it thoroughly.
3. Add a little bit of water or a binder which works for you until the mixture shapes well.

4. Put the dried flowers mixture on the bottom of the molds.
5. Stuff the molds with the mixture and once set for 5 minutes carefully take them out.
6. Let them dry for 24 hours.

**Anti-stress Milk Lavender Bath Bomb**

This bath bomb will turn the water in the bathtub into relaxing and stress releasing elixir. A gentle aroma of lavender will help to get rid of a headache and insomnia.

**Ingredients:**

1 cup baking soda

½ cup citric acid

1/4 cup sea salt (fine ground)

3 Tbsp. powdered milk

1 tbsp Cream of Tartar

2 Tbsp. grapeseed oil

1 Tsp. lavender essential oil or your fragrance oil

1 Tbsp. dried lavender flowers

INSTRUCTIONS:
1. Mix all the dry ingredients thoroughly in a large bowl.
2. Slowly add grapeseed oil mixed with your fragrance and combine it with the dry mixture until it creates a soft clump.
3. Add dried lavender flowers to the mixture.
4. Add your binder a little bit per time and mix quickly. Add your binder and mix until your mixture has the consistency similar to the wet sand and feels cool.
5. Mold your bath bombs.
6. Set aside for a few minutes.
7. Carefully take them out.
8. Let them try for 24 hours before using or packing.

## Mint Treasures

Mint bath bombs can refresh your mind, release all the negative thoughts, fill you up with energy.

**Ingredients:**

1 cup baking soda

½ cup citric acid

1 tbsp Cream of Tartar
2 Tbsp. grounded dried mint leaves (mint tea)
1.5 Tbsp. olive oil
12 drops mint essential oil or your fragrance oil

binder


INSTRUCTIONS:

1. Put grounded dried mint leaves into thermos cup and pour the cooking water over them.
2. Add boiling olive oil to mint tea and let the mixture cool down for 1 hour.
3. Mix baking soda with citric acid.
4. Add mint essential oil to the olive oil and then pour it into the dry mixture.
5. Start adding your binder after your dry ingredients are well combined with your oils.
6. Fill up the molds with the mixture and let these bath bombs dry for at

least 24 hours.

### Wake up Coffee Ylang Ylnag Bath Bomb

This DIY bath bomb with coffee and Ylang Ylang oil will give you a burst of energy. Wheat germ oil is going to make your skin soft. And coffee will boost your mood.

**Ingredients:**
1 cup baking soda
½ cup citric acid
3 Tbsp. cornstarch

1 tbsp. SLSA
2 Tbsp. wheat germ oil
1 Tbsp. coffee (grounded)
1 Tbsp. sea salt
15 drops Ylang Ylang essential oil
water or witch hazel or rubbing alcohol (a binder)

INSTRUCTIONS:
1. Mix citric acid and baking soda thoroughly.
2. Add 3 tbsp. cornstarch and mix it very well again.
3. Now add coffee and sea salt.
4. Then add 15 drops of Ylang Ylang essential oil to your oil.
5. Incorporate your liquid ingredients into your dry ones by slowly adding your oils and mixing well until your mixture gets very clumpy.
6. Add your binder and mix mix mix until your batter has the consistency of wet sand. If the mixture does not hold the shape when squeezed in a palm, then spray it a little bit with witch hazel or water.
7. Mold your bath bombs.
8. Carefully take them out and let them dry for at least 24 hours.

### Coffee and Cream Bath Bomb

If you are one of those people that love coffee so much that they could just bathe in it, then this recipe is made for you. Zero calorie and maximum sweetness! And since these bombs are made from fresh ingredients, it is recommended to use them during a week.

**Ingredients:**
1 cup baking soda

# The Simple Guide to Making Bath Bombs.

½ cup citric acid
1 Tbsp. powdered heavy cream
½ tbsp. powdered cinnamon

½ tbsp. ground coffee

1 tsp polysorbate 80
1.5 Tbsp. grapeseed oil
15 drops of your favorite essential oil or 1tsp fragrance oil
water or witch hazel or rubbing alcohol

colorant

INSTRUCTIONS:

1. Mix baking soda, citric acid and powdered heavy cream in a large bowl.
2. Add powdered cinnamon and ground coffee and mix thoroughly.
3. Slowly add grapeseed oil and mix it with the dry mixture until it has a clumpy consistency.
4. Add your favorite essential oil.
5. Sprinkle the mixture with a little bit of water and mix quickly. You can also use a different binder. It depends on your climate.
6. Mold your bath bombs.
7. Let the bath bombs stay in the molds for 10-15 minutes.
8. Take the bath bombs out carefully and let them dry for 24 hours.

**Chocolate Heaven**

These easy to make homemade fizzling bath bombs with essential oils are going to be a perfect mood booster for you and your loved ones. Natural ingredients will make your skin smooth and silky and your hair thick and glossy. Just try them out, and you won't regret!

**Ingredients:**

1 cup baking soda
½ cup citric acid
1 tbsp Cocoa powder

1 tbsp Milk Powder

1/8 cup Cornstarch

1 tbsp Cream of Tartar
2 Tbsp. coconut oil
5 drops cocoa essential oil
5 drops vanilla essential oil
water or witch hazel or rubbing alcohol

Colorant

INSTRUCTIONS:

1. Place the dry ingredients in a bowl and then whisk ingredients until mixed thoroughly.
2. Whisk liquid ingredients.
3. As you put the wet ingredients in the dry mixture whisk, mix it immediately to avoid clumps. Mix until you get a soft clump.
4. Add your binder a little bit per time and mix quickly. Add your binder and mix until your mixture has the consistency similar to the wet sand and feels cool.
5. Mold your bath bombs.
6. Set aside for a few minutes.
7. Carefully take them out.
8. Let them try for 24 hours before using or packing.
9. Store these bath bombs in an airtight container, jar or wrap them with plastic wrap.

The Simple Guide to Making Bath Bombs.

## Dead Sea Salt and Cosmetic Clay Bath Bomb

These universal bath bombs are perfect not only for relaxing after a long hard day they can be also helpful for a home manicure and pedicure procedures. The Dead Sea salt stimulates blood circulation, and cosmetic clay is rich in minerals. They are often used for face and hair masks, SPA procedures, etc. A hot bath with this bubbling fizzy bomb will nourish your skin and provide a SPA quality experience at home.

**Ingredients:**
8 tbsp. baking soda
4 Tbsp. citric acid
1 Tbsp. powdered milk
1 Tbsp. cornstarch
1 Tbsp. Dead Sea Salt
½ tbsp. black clay
½ tbsp. pink clay

2 Tbsp. rose infused oil

5 drops Eucalyptus essential oil or fragrance oil
rose petals (chopped)
water or witch hazel or rubbing alcohol as needed
colorant

INSTRUCTIONS:

1. Combine baking soda, citric acid, powdered milk, cornstarch and Dead Sea salt thoroughly. The mixture should not have any clumps.
2. Add rose infused oil mixed with the carrier oil and sprinkle the batter with some chopped rose petals. Mix until the mixture gets very clumpy.
3. Add your binder and mix until your mixture holds its shape very well and feels cool.
4. Separate the mixture into 3 bowls or containers.
5. Add black clay to the first container, pink one to the second one, and the third mixture will stay white.
6. Test the mixture if it shapes well. If it does not hold together like wet sand, then it is not ready. Slightly spray it with witch hazel or water and mix using your hands.
7. Mold your bath bombs layering with different colors.

## Anti-Cellulite Green Tea Bath Bombs

Taking a hot bath with Anti-Cellulite Green Tea Bath Bomb is going to improve your general skin condition and make cellulite less visible due to caffeine contained in the green tea. Green tea also has general antibacterial and anti-inflammatory properties. And the refreshing scent of eucalyptus essential oil will refresh your mind.

**Ingredients:**
1 cup baking soda
½ cup citric acid
¼ cup sea salt

¼ cornstarch

1 tbsp SLSA
3 Tbsp. jojoba oil
green tea as necessary
fragrance

colorant

INSTRUCTIONS:
1. Cook a little bit of water and pour it on green tea leaves.
2. Combine your presifted dry ingredients.
3. Mix jojoba oil with essential oil or your fragrance oil.
4. Now combine liquid and dry ingredients.
5. Once your mixture gets big clumps, you can start adding your binder (green tea). Add it very slowly and mix quickly.
6. When the mixture has the consistency of the wet sand, then it is ready to be molded.
7. Mold your bath bombs, carefully take them out and let them dry for at least 24 hours.

**Milky Bath Bomb**

**Ingredients:**
1 cup baking soda
1/2 cup powdered citric acid
1/4 cup cornstarch
1/8 cup finely ground Epsom salts
¼ cup powdered milk
½ tbsp. SLSA
2 tablespoons olive oil
1/2 tablespoons melted cocoa butter
Essential oils (6 - 10 drops) or fragrance oil

Colorant

INSTRUCTIONS:

1. Mix all the dry ingredients.
2. Add the liquid ingredients. Slowly add the olive oil and cocoa butter and gently mix the mixture using your hands. Add equal parts of witch hazel and lukewarm water using a spray bottle until the dough is solid enough to be compacted. Be careful when adding water as too much moisture will cause the mixture to begin fizzing.
3. Tip: Mix equal parts of witch hazel and water in the spray bottle before the procedure, then spritz the bath bomb ingredients two or three times. Stir the mixture and try squeezing it with your hands. If it does not hold together, add more liquid ingredients, and repeat.
4. Add color and fragrance. Choose the oil you want to use and add it to the mixture. If you want to experiment, then make a combination of two or more essential oil. However, keep in mind that you should not use more than 15 drops of essential oil to avoid skin irritation. You can add food colorant or some other skin safe colorant to the mixture to stay from a traditional white bath bomb.
5. Tip: Popular scents include lavender, rose, lilac, and eucalyptus. You can also use your favorite scent or experiment by combining one or multiple scents.
6. Put the dough mixture into molds. Firmly press the dough so that it sticks well and doesn't form cracks when dry.
7. Let the bath bombs dry out. Place the dough in the molds in a place that is cool and dry for at least 24 hours. When moisture has completely evaporated from the bath bombs, and they are already dry, carefully remove them from the molds.
8. Tip: If after 24 hours bath bombs are still moist, you can pop them out from the molds you are using and let the fizzes air dry for a few hours. Place them in a cool, dry area.
9. Store the bath bombs in a sealable container away from moisture.

**Vanilla Dream Skin Softening Bath Bombs with Vitamin E**

# The Simple Guide to Making Bath Bombs.

After a long hard day, you deserve to plunge into the hot bathtub with this vanilla fizz that will fill up the air with a wonderful aroma. Your skin is going to be smooth and silky.

**Ingredients:**

½ cup cornstarch

1 cup baking soda

½ citric acid

¼ Epsom Salts

1 tbsp Cream of Tartar

1 tbsp Milk Powder

2 tablespoons almond oil

½ tbsp. Vitamin E oil

Vanilla essential oil (6 -10 drops)

Coloring

binder

INSTRUCTIONS:

1. Gather all the ingredients.
2. Mix the dry ingredients first. Mix well and make sure there no clumps in your batter.
3. Add the liquid ingredients. Pour in avocado, almond oil, Vitamin E, and coconut oil into the mixture. Combine all the ingredients until you achieve a clumpy substance.

4. Mix in your preferred colors and scents. To make your bath bombs extra fancy, add in 6-10 drops of your favorite essential oil. Or you can try to mix multiple scents to create a unique combination. Add several drops of colorant to make your bath bombs colorful and stir the mixture well.
5. Add your binder slowly and mix vigorously until you have the consistency similar to the wet sand.

Tip: For a luxurious, relaxing bath, use lavender, chamomile, or lilac scents.

6. Mold your bath bombs.
7. Allow the bath bombs to dry.
8. Store the bath bombs. When the bath bombs feel dry, place them in an airtight container or a jar. Keep them away from moisture until they are ready to use. Enjoy your new bath bombs!

Tip: Use your new bath bombs within a few months to enjoy them before they crumble or decrease in quality.\

**Flower & Herb Bath Bombs**

This recipe includes dried herbs and flowers for a pretty, natural appearance.

**Ingredients:**

½ cup citric acid

1 cup bicarbonate of soda or baking soda

½ cup Cornstarch

½ cup Epsom Salt

# The Simple Guide to Making Bath Bombs.

2.5 tbsp sweet almond oil

Essential oils, several drops or fragrance oil

Dried herbs and flower petals

Water or a binder that works well for you

colorant (optional)

Cosmetic glitter (optional)

INSTRUCTIONS:
1. Gather all the ingredients.
2. Sift your dry ingredients and mix them well.
3. Cave in the center of the mixture using your fingers after mixing the two ingredients.
4. Pour in olive oil and essential oil and other accents of your choice. Then pour in the colorant and add dried herbs, or flower petals and cosmetic glitter (optional).

    Note: Do not use craft glitter. I recommend using cosmetic glitter.
5. Put in your rubber gloves on. Using your fingertips, mix the mixture in the bowl, making sure there are no lumps colorant in the mixture.

    Tip: Gloves are highly advisable as food colorant may color your skin.
6. Add your binder slowly and mix very fats to avoid a premature fizzing reaction.

    Tip: If the mixture still doesn't hold together after spraying, try spritzing once or twice more. Continue this until you achieve a wet sand-like consistency.
7. After spraying, the mixture will start to harden. Quickly pick up small handfuls of the mixture, pressing it firmly into your preferred molds.
8. They should be dry the next day. Once dry, you can pack your bath bombs and use them!

**Orange Zest Bath Bomb**

In this recipe, we are going to use liquid Polysorbate 80. It will help to avoid oil stains in your bathtub. You do not have to use any colorant because orange peel powder will give your bath bombs this light creamy orange color. A fresh, invigorating smell will fill up your bathroom and will revitalize your spirit.

**Ingredients:**
1 cup baking soda

½ cup citric acid

1 tbsp rice powder

1 tbsp orange or grapefruit peel powder

1 tbsp Cream of Tartar

1 tbsp cocoa butter

½ tbsp. grapeseed oil

1 tsp liquid Polysorbate-80

10 drops of orange essential oil

Coloring

Your binder as needed

Dried orange zest or dried orange pieces (for decorating)

INSTRUCTIONS:

1. In a large bowl mix baking soda, citric acid, rice powder and orange peel powder. To avoid clumps, you can grind the dry ingredients in a coffee grinder, or sieve them through. Either of these procedures will make the bath bomb texture fine and homogenous.
2. Melt the cocoa butter in a microwave. Let the melted cocoa butter cool down until the room temperature.
3. Mix the melted cocoa butter with Polysorbate-80 and grapeseed oil.
4. Now slowly add oil mixture to the dry ingredients. Mix well until it has a very clumpy consistency.
5. Add your binder until your mixture has the consistency of the wet sand or fluffy snow and holds together when squeezed in your palm.
6. When the right consistency is achieved, you can add 10 drops of orange essential oil and mix it one more time.
7. Sprinkle the molds with orange zest or dried orange pieces.
8. Mold your bath bombs.
9. Let them dry in the molds for 24 hours.
10. Carefully take the bath bombs out and wrap them in a plastic wrap or store them in an airtight container or jar.

**Chia Seeds Bath Bomb**

# The Simple Guide to Making Bath Bombs.

Chia seeds are well known for their health benefits, and many people include this product in their diet. But these wonder seeds also have many benefits for our skin as chia seeds are rich in Vitamin E which is easily absorbed by our body. This ingredient, when added to a basic bath bomb recipe, can make your skin smooth and well nourished.

**Ingredients:**
1 cup baking powder

½ cup citric acid

¼ cup tbsp rice powder

2 tbsp pink clay

2 tbsp chia seeds powder

2 tbsp apricot seeds oil

10 drops lavender essential oil

1 tbsp lavender seeds

Water or witch hazel or rubbing alcohol as needed

INSTRUCTIONS:
1. In a large bowl mix all the dry ingredients except lavender seeds. If you want your bath bombs to have a fine texture, then you should sieve all the dry ingredients or grind them in a coffee grinder.
2. Now slowly pour in olive oil and mix thoroughly. The mixture should have the clumpy consistency. Add your binder to achieve the wet sand-like consistency. If the mixture feels too dry, you can spray it with some water or witch hazel. Keep in mind, that if you add too many liquids, then the fizzing reaction between citric acid and baking soda might start prematurely. That is why add just a little bit of your liquids at a time and right away mix it in quick moves.
3. Add essential oil and mix one more time. You can also combine your essential oil with your carrier oils first.
4. Now sprinkle the mixture with lavender seeds and mix.
5. Mold your bath bombs.
6. Let the bath bombs dry for 2-3 hours, and then carefully take them out and let them dry for 24 hours.

**Disinfecting and Deodorizing Toilet Bath Bombs**
If you want to deodorize and naturally disinfect your toilet, then make these toilet bath bombs. It is a simple way to freshen up your toilet. Just put one of those fizzes in the toilet watch it being cleaned up.

**Ingredients:**

1 cup baking soda
½ cup citric acid
½ cups borax
zip-top bag
water
10 drops lemon essential oil
10 drops peppermint essential oil
10 drops eucalyptus essential oil

INSTRUCTIONS:

1. Mix baking soda, borax and citric acid in a zip-top back. Knead the mixture well to avoid clumps.
2. Then open the bag and spray the mixture with a little bit of water. Knead the dough well. Repeat several times until the mixture has the consistency of the wet sand. When you squeeze the zip-top bag, you should see that the bath bomb mixture holds together. Be aware that if you add too much water, you might end up with the crumbling final product.
3. Add 30 drops of pure essential oils and mix the dough again.
4. When the necessary consistency is achieved, you can stuff your molds with the mixture. Make sure you pack the molds tight.
5. Let the toilet fresheners stay in the molds for 24 hours until completely dry. Then you can take them out and store in an airtight container or a jar. If you notice that the smell of essential oils is not strong enough, then you might want to add a few drops on of the toilet bath bombs before dropping it into the toilet.

**Raspberry and Vanilla Cream Bath Bomb**

This raspberry bath bomb has a fresh fruity aroma and contains a freeze-dried raspberry powder which is rich in A, C, and E and has many skin-loving benefits. The raspberry also has a soft pink and creamy color because of the organic raspberry powder so you would not need a colorant at all.

**Ingredients:**
1 cup baking soda
½ cup citric acid
½ cup Epsom salt
2 tbsp cornstarch

# The Simple Guide to Making Bath Bombs.

2 tbsp organic freeze-dried raspberry powder
2 tbsp apricot kernel oil
10 drops raspberry essential oil or fragrance oil
10 drops vanilla cream fragrance oil
hazel witch or water or rubbing alcohol in a spray bottle as needed

INSTRUCTIONS:

1. In a large bowl mix citric acid, baking soda, Epsom salt, cornstarch. Break up the clumps with your hands if necessary.
2. Mix apricot kernel oil with the essential oil and fragrance oil.
3. Add oils to the dry mixture. Make sure that you add a little bit of the liquids at a time and mix quickly. You will notice that the mixture is going to get clumpy.
4. Now divide the mixture into two parts. Add raspberry powder to the first one to get a gentle pink color.
5. Make a consistency test. Squeeze a little bit of the pink mixture with your palm. If the mixture holds its shape but is still very easy to break, then it is time to add your binder. If the mixture is too dry, then spray it with witch hazel or water. Be careful with adding water or witch hazel, because too much liquid may cause the fizzing reaction between citric acid and baking soda. The consistency you are looking for is the one which is similar to the wet sand. It should hold its shape well. So when you make a clump and drop it in your bowl with the batter, you should be able to pick it up.
6. Then make a consistency test with the white mixture. If the consistency of the bath bomb mixture is not right, then you should give the mixture a few sprays of water or witch hazel.
7. Now it is time to fill up the molds. Put a little bit of the pink mixture and then add a white one on top of it and pack your molds.
9. Let the bath bombs air dry overnight and then pack them in your favorite way.

**Vanilla Cake Bath Bomb**

**Ingredients:**

1 cup baking soda

½ cup citric acid

2 tbsp buttermilk powder

1 tbsp. Dead Sea salt

¼ cup cornstarch

1 tbsp cream of tartar

3 tsp. Shea butter (melted)

1 tbsp olive oil

Small spray bottle of Witch Hazel or water or rubbing alcohol (depends on the humidity)

15 drops Vanilla essential oil or fragrance oil

Orange coloring

Sprinkles

¼ lb. goat's milk soap base (melted) + colorant for a drizzle

1. Combine all of your dry ingredients in a large mixing bowl. Use your fingers to break up any clumps.
2. Melt Shea butter in a saucepan or microwave until it is liquid and mix it with your olive oil and your fragrance.
3. Add the oils to the dry mixture. Mix thoroughly.
4. Spray a small amount of witch hazel to the mixture until it holds together when you scoop it with your hands. If the mixture crumbles easily, add another 1-2 spray of witch hazel. Refrain from spraying too much; it will cause premature fizzing.
5. Place the mixture into the cake mold. Press firmly.
6. Leave the mixture in the molds for at least a few hours or overnight.
7. Melt the goat's milk soap base and mix in your colorant and drizzle it over the cake bath bombs.
8. Add sprinkles immediately. Let the goat's milk soap set for at least 10 minutes.

## Pinky Clouds

**Ingredients:**

1 cup baking soda

½ cup Citric Acid

½ cup pink cosmetic clay

¼ cup powdered Milk

1 tbsp. bath salt or Epsom salt

½ cup rose petals (dried) cut into small pieces

One tsp. water

3-4 tsp. Almond oil

15-20 drops rose oil or fragrance oil

1 tsp of water (you might need more or a little bit less depending on your humidity)

INSTRUCTIONS:

1. Combine baking soda, citric acid, cosmetic clay, powdered milk, and bath salt in a large mixing bowl.
2. Add the dried rose petals.
3. In a separate bowl, mix water, almond oil, and rose oil. Mix thoroughly.
4. Pour the wet ingredients into the dry mixture. Stir to incorporate everything together until the mixture shapes well when squeezed in your palms.
5. Mold your bath bombs.

6. Carefully pop them out from the molds and let them dry on a towel for at least a few hours before using or wrapping them as gifts.

# The Simple Guide to Making Bath Bombs.

**Cinnamon Latte Bath Bomb**

**Ingredients:**

3 1/2 cups baking soda

2 tbsp Sodium Lauryl Sulfoacetate (SLSA)

2 cups citric Acid

3 tbs. powdered heavy cream

1 oz. coffee butter (melted)

6 ml. cinnamon essential oil

5 ml. espresso fragrance oil

10 ml. polysorbate 80

1 tbsp. cocoa powder

orange mica or orange food coloring

Witch Hazel or water or rubbing alcohol in a spray bottle

Coffee beans for decoration

INSTRUCTIONS:

1. Mix baking soda, citric acid, SLSA and goat's milk powder in a large mixing bowl.
2. Place coffee butter in a small microwavable container. Microwave for at least 15-20 seconds.
3. Add your fragrance oils and polysorbate 80 into the melted butter. Combine thoroughly.
4. Gradually combine the butter mixture into the dry mix.
5. Evenly split the mixture into three containers.

6. In one of the containers, add the cocoa powder. Mix well. In the second container, add the orange mica. Mix well. Leave the third container uncolored.
7. Spray each container with a small amount of your binder and mix quickly. Continue spraying until the mixture will hold its shape.
8. Place a few coffee beans in the center of the molds. Fill the mold half full with a small amount of white bath bomb mixture, covering the coffee beans. Press gently with your fingers.
9. Place the brown bath bomb mixture over the white mixture. Set aside.
10. In the opposite half of the bath bomb mold, place a little amount of orange bath bomb mixture. Then add more of the white bath bomb mixture over the orange mix. You shouldn't pack your bath bombs too tight if you want them to float.
11. Close the molds while applying direct pressure to the edges instead of the center.
12. Let the bath bombs dry for 24 hours or longer.

Note: The shelf life of these bath bombs is about two months due to the powdered goat's milk.

**Velvet Sky**

**Ingredients:**

2 cups baking soda

1.5 cup citric acid

1/2 cup black sea salt

1 tbsp white sea salt (coarse)

½ cup cornstarch

1 tbsp cream of tartar

1 tbsp SLSA

2 tbsp grapeseed oil

2 tbsp melted coconut oil

10 drops lavender essential oil or fragrance oil

1 tbsp Polysorbate 80

coloring

Witch hazel or water or rubbing alcohol in a spray bottle

INSTRUCTIONS:

1. In a separate container, mix your carrier oils, Polysorbate 80, and the lavender essential oil. Mix well to incorporate the ingredients.
2. Sift all of your dry ingredients in a large bowl and mix well.
3. Pour the oil mixture into the dry mixture and combine thoroughly. Break all of those little clumps with your hands, a spatula or a whisk. You can also use a pastry cutter to make it easier.
4. Spray the mixture with a binder of your choice until you get the right consistency. The texture should be similar to wet sand that holds its shape when pressed.
5. Sprinkle a little amount of the coarse sea salt into the bottom of each mold. Then overfill your round molds as much as you can and then push two parts together.
6. Continue to fill each mold with the mixture.
7. Let the bath bombs dry for overnight.

**Healing Freshness**

**Ingredients:**

1 cup baking soda

1/2 cup citric acid

1 tbsp blue clay

1 tbsp. Epsom salt or bath salt

1 tbsp tapioca starch

1 tbsp. olive oil

1 tbsp Sweet Almond oil

15 drops Peppermint essential oil

15 drops Eucalyptus essential oil

Binder as needed

green coloring

dried peppermint leaves or peppermint tea

Bath bomb molds

INSTRUCTIONS:

1. Combine presifted dry ingredients in a large mixing bowl and mix thoroughly.
2. Mix your oils and gradually pour them in into the mixture while mixing. Continue doing so until all the clumps are gone.
3. Add green food colorant and mix well. If you want a deeper green color, you would need to add more coloring.
4. Add dried peppermint leaves or peppermint tea.
5. Give the mixture a few sprays of your binder. Mix well. Spray more if needed or until you get the perfect texture. The consistency of a good bath bomb mixture should be similar to the one of the wet sand.
6. Mold your bath bombs.
7. Let them dry for 24 hours or longer.

**Sweet Grape Bath Bomb**

**Ingredients:**

1 cup baking soda

½ cup. citric acid

1/8 cup cornstarch

1/4 cup Epsom salts

1 tbsp Milk Powder

1 tbsp Cream of Tartar

1.5-2 tbsp grapeseed powder

2 tbsp grapeseed oil

Binder as needed

2 tsp. sweet grape fragrance oil

Sugar sprinkles for decoration

INSTRUCTIONS:

## The Simple Guide to Making Bath Bombs.

1. In a large mixing bowl, mix all the dry ingredients (salt, baking soda, cornstarch, and grape seed powder, citric acid.
2. In a separate bowl, mix the wet ingredients (water, essential oil, grape seed oil and food coloring).
3. Pour the wet mixture into the dry mixture. Mix well. The consistency should be similar to wet sand.
4. Combine thoroughly until the color is even. Once the color is even, it is an indication that it is already to be molded. The mixture should hold together well.
5. Sprinkle your bath bomb molds with sugar sprinkles or other decoration pieces.
6. Mold your bath bombs.
7. Carefully remove one side of the ball molder. Let it dry for 1-2 hours. Then take the bath bombs out and let them dry for 24 hours.
8. Make sure that the bath bombs are dry before taking them all out.

**Ocean Breeze Bath Bomb**

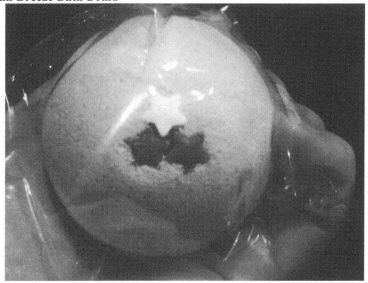

**Ingredients:**
1 cup baking soda
1/2 cup citric acid
1 tbsp. cornstarch
2 tbsp bath salt or Epsom Salts
½ tbsp. SLSA
2 tbsp Milk Powder
5-6 drops blue coloring
1 tbsp. coconut oil
½ tbsp. Sweet Almond oil
5 drops Geranium essential oil
5 drops Lime essential oil
5 drops Coriander essential oil
5 drops Eucalyptus essential oil
Binder as necessary

INSTRUCTIONS:

1. In a large mixing bowl, combine baking soda, citric acid, cornstarch, bath salt, milk powder, and SLSA. Combine all the dry ingredients thoroughly.
2. Add the wet ingredients. Whisk thoroughly to break any clumps in the mixture.
3. Spray a little amount of your binder (for example water) and mix mix mix. The consistency of the mixture should be similar to damp sand. Test the mixture by squeezing it together in your hands. It should be able to hold its shape.
4. Mold your bath bombs.
5. Carefully remove one half of the bath bomb mold. Tip it over and gently remove the other half of the mold.
6. Let the bath bombs dry on top of a clean towel. Take a relaxing bath and enjoy!

**Honey and Grapefruit Bath Bomb**

**Ingredients:**

1 cup baking soda

1/2 cup citric acid

1 tbsp Cornstarch

1 tbsp Epsom Salts

4 tbsp Milk Powder

1.5-2 tbsp. olive oil

½ tsp Polysorbate 80

1 tsp. liquid honey or 1 tbsp honey powder

10 drops grapefruit essential oil

10 drops Honey Fragrance Oil or Honey Myrtle Essential oil

Colorant

Binder of your choice as needed

INSTRUCTIONS:

1. In a mixing bowl, mix baking soda, citric acid, milk powder and Epsom salts. Whisk thoroughly.
2. In a separate bowl, mix olive oil, liquid honey, polysorbate 80 and essential oils. Stir well.
3. Slowly add the wet ingredients to dry mixture. The consistency should be crumbly.

4. Now spray the mixture with witch hazel or water or rubbing alcohol (depends on the humidity) and mix quickly with your hands. Continue to spray until the mixture gets that wet sand consistency. Once the mixture can hold its shape and sticks together without crumbling, it means that your mixture is ready.
5. Place your bath bomb mixture into bath bomb molds.
6. Remove the bath bombs gently and place them on a baking sheet to dry and harden for at least 24 hours before moving or packaging them.

## Tropical Island

**Ingredients:**

1 cup baking soda

1/2 cup citric acid

1/2 cup cornstarch

1/2 cup Epsom salts

1 tbsp SLSA

2.5 tbsp. coconut oil

5 drops Coconut essential oil

5 drops Mango essential oil

5 drops Awapuhi essential oil

5 drops Pineapple essential oil (you can also use a fragrance oil instead)

Yellow coloring

Green coloring

Witch hazel or water or rubbing alcohol in a spray bottle or use a dropper to add your binder

INSTRUCTIONS:

1. Combine all the dry ingredients in a large mixing bowl. Stir well. Set aside.
2. Mix the coconut oil, 1 tsp water, essential oils. Mix well to combine the ingredients thoroughly.

3. Gently spray the dry ingredients with the liquid ingredients, while mixing at the same time. Mix until the texture is that of damp sand.
4. Divide the mixture into three parts and place them into different containers or bowls. Add green colorant to the first mixture, yellow to the second one, and the third one will be simply white.
5. Scoop a little bit of the first of your bath bomb mixture and place into your bath bomb mold. Then add the other ones. Repeat until the bath bomb molds are full. In this way, you will get a nice colorful pattern for the bath bombs. Leave them for 10 minutes to set.
6. Carefully take out your ready bath bombs from the molds. Place them on top of a clean, dry towel. Leave them overnight to harden.

**Peppermint Bath Bomb**

**Ingredients:**

1 cup baking soda

½ cup citric acid

¼ cup cornstarch

1 tbsp. green cosmetic clay

1.5 tbsp Macadamia oil or coconut oil

green coloring

14 drops peppermint essential oil

INSTRUCTIONS:

1. In a mixing bowl, mix r all the dry ingredients (baking soda, citric acid, green cosmetic clay, and cornstarch). Combine thoroughly.
2. Separate your mixture into two bowls.
3. In one bowl, add green food coloring. Mix well.
4. Add peppermint essential oil to the two bowls and mix thoroughly.
5. Gradually pour in Macadamia oil into each bowl while mixing. The texture should be similar to damp sand.
6. Fill in your molds with your bath bomb mixture with a combination of the green and white peppermint mix.
7. Mold your bath bombs.
8. Let the bath bombs dry for at least 24 hours before using or packaging them.

# The Simple Guide to Making Bath Bombs.

**Autumn Gifts**

**Ingredients:**

1 cup baking soda

1/8 cup Epsom salts

½ cup citric acid

1/4 cup powdered milk

1 tbsp Cream of Tartar

1 tbsp. olive oil

1 tbsp. Calendula oil

5 drops fig essential oil

5 drops Pumpkin Spice fragrance oil

5 drops ginger essential oil

5 drops balsam fir essential oil

2 drops eucalyptus essential oil

Binder as needed

INSTRUCTIONS:

1. Start by mixing all the dry ingredients in a large bowl.
2. In a small bowl, mix your oils.
3. Pour the magnesium oil mixture into the dry ingredients slowly while mixing thoroughly. Adding the liquid ingredients too fast will cause premature fizzing.
4. Slowly add your binder and continue mixing until the texture is similar to damp sand and can hold its shape when you squeeze it.
5. Once the mixture is ready to mold you can start filling up your bath molds
6. Let the bath bombs dry for 24 hours.

**Chamomile and Bergamot Relaxation Bath Bomb**

**Ingredients:**

1 cup of baking soda

1 tbsp cup of cornstarch

1/2 cup of citric acid

2 tbsp Milk Powder

1 tbsp SLSA

1 tsp. rice bran oil

1 tbsp avocado oil

8 drops Roman Chamomile essential oil

8 drops of lavender essential oil

4 drops Bergamot essential oil

Yellow colorant (or 1 tbsp of lemon peel powder)

Witch hazel or water or rubbing alcohol 50-91 % in a spray bottle

INSTRUCTIONS:

1. Begin by mixing all the dry ingredients into a large mixing bowl. Combine thoroughly.
2. Slowly pour in the rice bran oil and essential oils into the dry ingredients while mixing.
3. Add your colorant and mix well.
4. Using a spray bottle with water, spritz a little amount into the bath bomb mixture slowly. Do not add too much water as it will cause premature fizzing. The texture should be slightly similar to damp sand.
5. Fill up your bath bomb molds with the mixture and push them together.
6. Carefully remove them from the molds or the wax paper.
7. Let them dry for at least 24 hours. Enjoy!

**Ginger and Honey Bath Bomb**

**Ingredients:**

1 cup baking soda

1/4 cup citric acid

1/8 cup cornstarch

1 tbsp Honey Powder

1 tbsp Cream of Tartar

1.5 tbsp Calendula oil or Grapeseed oil

10 drops Ginger root essential oil

10 drops Honey fragrance oil

Gold Mica

Witch hazel or water in a spray bottle or rubbing alcohol (1 -2 tsp water)

INSTRUCTIONS:

1. In a large bowl, mix baking soda, citric acid, honey powder cream of tartar and cornstarch.
2. Then slowly add the ginger essential oil and the calendula oil to the mixture. Mix using your hands to get rid of clumps.
3. Add golden mica and mix thoroughly.
4. Slowly add your binder and mix quickly.
5. Once the mixture is ready, and their texture is like that of damp sand, you can now fill your bath bomb molds.
6. Gently remove them from the molds. Let your bath bombs dry for at least 24 hours.

**Mulled Wine in Your Bath Tub**

**Ingredients:**

1/2 cup cornstarch

2 cup baking soda

1/4 cup Epsom salt

1 cup citric acid

4 tbsp Milk Powder

3.5 tbsp coconut oil

20 drops Mulled Wine Fragrance Oil Concentrate

If you do not have Mulled Wine Fragrance Oil then use the following essential oils:

5 drops clove essential oil

5 drops cinnamon essential oil

5 drops anise essential oil

5 drops orange essential oil

Red coloring

Witch hazel or water or rubbing alcohol in a spray bottle

Rosebuds or petals for decoration (dried)

INSTRUCTIONS:

1. In a mixing bowl, combine the dry ingredients thoroughly.

2. Slowly add fragrance oil or essential oils blend into the dry mixture as well as coconut oil. Mix well.
3. Add a few drops of your colorant to the mixture while mixing at the same time.
4. Spray a small amount of water into the mixture until the texture is barely moist. Do not add too much as it will cause the bath bomb mixture to fizz prematurely.
5. Sprinkle the bath bomb molds with rose buds or petals.
6. Mold your bath bombs.
7. Remove them gently from the molds and let your bath fizzies dry for at least 24 hours. Use and enjoy.

# The Simple Guide to Making Bath Bombs.

**Strawberry and Vanilla Bath Bomb**

**Ingredients:**

1/4 cup Epsom salts

1 cup Baking Soda

1/4 cup Cornstarch

1/2 cup Citric Acid

1 tbsp Cream of Tartar

1 ½-2 tbsp. apricot kernel oil

10 drops Strawberry fragrance oil

5 drops Vanilla essential oil

5 drops Musk essential oil

With hazel or water or rubbing alcohol in a spray bottle

INSTRUCTIONS:

1. Start by combining all the dry ingredients and sifting them.
2. Add the apricot kernel oil and essential oils into the dry ingredients and mix very well.
3. Spray a small amount of witch hazel or water into the mixture until the texture holds together and can hold its shape when formed.
4. Place the mixture into the molds.
5. Allow them to dry for at least 24 hours before using.

## Japanese Garden

**Ingredients:**
1 tbsp pink clay

1/2 cup citric acid

1 cup baking soda

¼ cup powdered milk

2 ½ tbsp. liquid coconut oil

10 drops Japanese Cherry Blossom fragrance oil

5 drops neroli essential oil

5 drops Cherry Blossom fragrance oil

Spray bottle with witch hazel

INSTRUCTIONS:

1. In a large mixing bowl, add the dry ingredients: pink clay baking soda, citric acid, and powdered milk.
2. Add the liquid ingredients (coconut oil and essential oil) into the dry mixture. Stir well.
3. Spray a little amount of your binder when the mixture starts clumping. The mixture should be similar to damp sand.
4. Scoop the bath bomb mixture and place them into the bath bomb molds.
5. Carefully pop them out from the molds. Let them dry for at least 24 hours before using or packaging them.

## Floral Patterns

# The Simple Guide to Making Bath Bombs.

**Ingredients:**

1 cup baking soda

1/2 cup citric acid

1/2 cup cornstarch

1/2 cup Epsom salts

1 tbsp Cream of Tartar

2 tbsp Jojoba oil

10 drops. rose essential oil

5drops lavender essential oil

5 drops Geranium essential oil

5 drops Ylang Ylang essential oil

You can use 6 g Fragrance oil instead of essential oils

Red coloring

Dried lavender

Dried rose buds and petals

Witch Hazel or water or rubbing alcohol

INSTRUCTIONS:
1. In a large bowl, combine all the dry ingredients: baking soda, citric acid, cornstarch, cream of tartar, Epsom salts, and dried lavender and rose flowers.
2. In a separate bowl, combine the wet ingredients: water, oils, and your coloring.

3. Slowly pour in the content of the liquid bowl into the dry mixture, mixing as you go.
4. Continue to mix until the mixture starts to resemble wet sand. It should be able to hold together when squeezed. If it does not, you can spritz the mixture with witch hazel or water until you get the right consistency.
5. Place the mixture into the molds and pack them tightly.
6. Allow them to dry for 24 hours before using.

## Hibiscus and Pink Himalayan Salt Bath Bomb

**Ingredients:**

1cup baking soda

¼ cup fine grain Pink Himalayan Salt

1/2 cup Citric Acid

1 tsp Hibiscus Powder

1 tbsp Milk Powder

1 tsp calendula oil

1 tbsp avocado oil

10 drops Lavender Essential Oil

5 drops Hibiscus essential oil

5 drops orange essential oil

Dried hibiscus petals (Hibiscus tea)

Witch hazel or water or rubbing alcohol in a spray bottle

INSTRUCTIONS:

1. Mix the dry ingredients. Set aside.
2. Add the oils and the essential oils. Mix well.
3. Add dried Hibiscus petals.
4. Lightly spray the dry mixture with witch hazel to moisten. Do not add too much. The mixture should stick together rather than crumbling.
5. Once the mixture has the right consistency, place it in the molds.
6. Let the mixture dry for a few minutes and carefully take them out from the molds.
7. Allow them to dry on the top of a towel for at least 24 hours before using or storing in an airtight container.

The Simple Guide to Making Bath Bombs.

# Honey, Oatmeal & Milk Bath Bomb

Ingredients:
  1 cup Baking Soda
  1/2 cup Citric Acid
  1 tbsp Cream of Tartar
  1.5 tbsp Milk Powder
  1 tbsp Epsom Salts
  1 tbsp Colloidal Oats
  1 tbsp Honey Powder
  1.5-2 tbsp grapeseed oil
  3 ml Oatmeal and Honey Fragrance oil
  2 tsp water (If you live in a humid climate you can use rubbing alcohol 70% and higher)

INSTRUCTIONS:
1. Sift all of your dry ingredients in a large mixing bowl and mix them well.
2. Mix your oils and add them to your dry mixture. Mix well to incorporate all the ingredients.
3. Add your binder a little bit per time. You can use a dropper to make it easier for you. Mix very fast, so your mix does not activate prematurely.
4. When your mixture has damp sand-like consistency stop adding your water or whatever binder you choose to use.
5. Mold your bath bombs.
6. Take them out and let your bath bombs dry at least 24 hours before packaging or using them.

### Recipes for Children

Sometimes it is difficult to make your kids to take a bath. That is why we have prepared these beautiful and colorful DIY bath bombs recipes for kids. You can even make them together with your children. These bath bombs will explode with aromatic essential oils and bright fuzziness. That will make kids excited about taking a bath. These homemade organic bath bombs will turn their bathing routine into a joyful game with all these bubbling, fizzing and color exploding. At the same time, this process can calm them down, relax and prepare for the bedtime. So here they are, simple, safe and easy to follow recipes for DIY organic bath bombs for kids.

### Colorful Easter Egg Bath Bomb

Children love to look for Easter eggs so much. Here is an idea! Make these amazing Easter egg bath bombs, make a creative gift-wrapping for them and let your kids find these eggs. These bath bombs' colorant and festive shape will get your kids interested and excited. It might become your new family tradition. So, let us get started.

**Ingredients:**

1 cup baking soda

½ cup citric acid

½cup cornstarch

¼ cup Epsom salt

2 tbsp. of olive oil

¼ Tsp. German chamomile oil

¼ Tsp. Blue Tansy oil

3 types of coloring

water as needed

large Easter egg molds

INSTRUCTIONS:

1. Mix dry ingredients in a large bowl.
2. Combine olive oil, essential oils and food coloring.
3. Then slowly add dry mixture to liquid ingredients and mix well until it clumps well. If not, then add a little bit of water.
4. Prepare three mixtures with different coloring. Use gloves to avoid colorant of your hands.
5. First, press one of the bath bomb mixtures into the mold.

6. Then add the mixture of another color.

7. Sprinkle the third mixture on the top of the second one and continue alternating your colors until you overfill both parts of your molds. Push them together.

8. Take these bath bombs out carefully and let them dry at least for 24 hours.

**Good Night My Little Star**

In this recipe, we are going to use lavender oil which is going to help your kids calm, relax and prepare them for a nice good night's sleep.

**Ingredients:**

1 cup baking soda

1/4 cup cornstarch

1/8 cup citric acid

1 tbsp Cream of Tartar

1.5 tbsp. Olive oil

1 tsp of lavender essential oil

2 tbsp. of dried chamomile

colorant (optional)

water as needed (or any other binder you like to use)

INSTRUCTIONS:

1. Mix all the dry ingredients thoroughly.
2. Combine olive oil with essential oil and colorant (optional).
3. Slowly add olive oil and essential oil to the dry mixture and mix until it sticks together and shapes well.
4. Slowly add your binder and ix quickly until you have the consistency similar to damp sand.
5. Mold your bath bombs.
6. Let them dry.

7. Scoop them out and wrap bath bombs in a plastic wrap or use a plastic container for storage.

# The Simple Guide to Making Bath Bombs.

**Milk and Honey Bath Bomb with a Surprise**

This bath bomb releases a wonderful sweet smell and kids love to watch the way it fizzes the water. It also has a calming and relaxing effect. But we wanted to make it really special. So, go on and get some cute toys and put them into this healthy Milk and Honey bath bomb. You can surprise your kids with these mini gifts on some special occasions.

**Ingredients:**

1 cup baking soda

¼ cup cornstarch

½ cup citric acid

¼ powdered milk

2 tsp avocado oil or shea butter or cocoa butter

1 Tbsp. warm honey

1 Tsp. Mandarin essential oil or Milk and Honey Fragrance oil

Binder (I use about 1-2 tsp water depending on the humidity)

INSTRUCTIONS:

1. Mix the baking soda, citric acid, corn starch and powdered milk.
2. Melt shea butter (cocoa butter) and add warm honey and olive oil.
3. Add liquid ingredients to the dry mixture.
4. Add essential oil and mix very well until everything is well incorporated.
5. Slowly add your binder and mix everything until it has the consistency of wet sand and holds together when you make a ball.
6. Put a little bit of mixture into the mold, press it firmly and then place a surprise toy. After that, fill up the mold with the mixture leaving clean edges.
7. Let the mixture stay in the molds for a few minutes and then take them out.
8. Let the bath bombs dry overnight.

## Conclusion

Thank you for reading my book. I hope that this guide has helped you in your bath bomb-making journey. If you have, any questions regarding bath bombs you can join my group on Facebook where I gladly answer all the questions and troubleshoot your recipes.

I also have a bath and body related blog, which you may find useful.

If you could take a minute and leave an honest review, I would be very thankful.

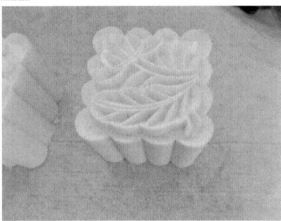

Manufactured by Amazon.ca
Bolton, ON